For my father, Robert French,
and for Brian and Jennifer Chandler,
Les Hughes (in memory)
and for Mavis Hughes and Jane Hill

First published in Great Britain in 2002 by
Frances Lincoln Limited, 4 Torriano Mews
Torriano Avenue, London NW5 2RZ

British Library Cataloguing in Publication Data
available on request

ISBN 0-7112-1858-7

Printed in Singapore

1 3 5 7 9 8 6 4 2

EASTER

FIONA FRENCH

With words from the Authorized Version of
KING JAMES BIBLE

FRANCES LINCOLN

When they heard that Jesus was coming to Jerusalem, people took branches of palm trees, and went forth to meet him, and cried, "Hosanna: Blessed is the King of Israel that cometh in the name of the Lord!"

Now when the even was come,
Jesus sat down with the twelve.
And as they did eat, Jesus took bread,
and blessed and brake it, and gave
to them and said, "Take, eat: this is
my body."

And he took the cup, and when he
had given thanks he gave it to them:
and they all drank of it.

Then cometh Jesus with them unto a place called Gethsemane. And Judas, one of the twelve, came, and with him a great multitude with swords and staves from the chief priests and elders of the people.

Now he that betrayed him gave them a sign, saying, "Whomsoever I shall kiss, that same is he: hold him fast." And he came to Jesus and said, "Hail, master", and kissed him. Then they laid hands on Jesus, and took him.

Λnd when they had bound him,
   they led him away and delivered
him to Pontius Pilate the governor.
And the governor asked him, saying,
"Art thou the King of the Jews?"
And Jesus said unto him, "Thou sayest."

But the chief priests
and elders persuaded the
multitude that they should destroy
Jesus. When Pilate saw that he could
prevail nothing, he took water, and
washed his hands, saying,
"I am innocent of the blood of
this just person. See ye to it."

Then the soldiers of the governor took Jesus into the common hall. And they stripped him and put on him a scarlet robe. And when they had plaited a crown of thorns, they put it upon his head, and a reed in his right hand: and they bowed the knee before him and mocked him, saying, "Hail, King of the Jews!"

And as they came out, they found
a man of Cyrene, Simon by name:
him they compelled to bear Jesus' cross.
And they were come unto a place called
Golgotha, that is to say, a place of a skull.

And they crucified him.

When the even was come,
there came a rich man
of Arimathaea named Joseph,
who also himself was Jesus' disciple.
He went to Pilate and begged the body
of Jesus. And when Joseph had taken
the body, he wrapped it in a clean linen cloth
and laid it in his own new tomb, and he rolled
a great stone to the door of the sepulchre,
and departed.

Now upon the first day of the week, very early in the morning, Mary Magdalene and the other Mary came unto the sepulchre, and found the stone rolled away. They entered in, and found not the body of the Lord Jesus.

And behold, two men stood by them in shining garments, and said unto them, "Why seek ye the living among the dead? He is not here, but is risen."

Then the same day at evening, when the disciples were assembled, came Jesus and saith unto them, "Peace be unto you." But Thomas, one of the twelve, was not with them when Jesus came. The other disciples said unto him, "We have seen the Lord." But he said, "Except I shall see in his hands the print of the nails, and thrust my hand into his side, I will not believe."

After eight days
his disciples were within, and
Thomas with them: then came Jesus
and stood in the midst. Then saith he
to Thomas, "Behold my hands, and reach
hither thy hand and thrust it into my side,
and be not faithless, but believing."
And Thomas said, "My Lord and my God!"

Jesus shewed himself again to
   the disciples at the sea of Tiberias.
   He saith unto them, "Children,
have ye any meat?" They answered him,
"No." And he said, "Cast the net
on the right side of the ship, and ye
shall find." They cast therefore,
and were not able to draw it for
the multitude of fishes.

As soon then as they were
come to land, they saw a fire
of coals there, and fish laid
thereon, and bread. Jesus saith
unto them, "Come and dine."
And none of the disciples durst
ask him, "Who art thou?"
knowing that it was the Lord.

And he led them out as far as to Bethany, and he lifted up his hands and blessed them. And it came to pass, while he blessed them, he was parted from them and carried up into heaven. And they worshipped him, and returned to Jerusalem with great joy.